AF316810

SPARKING CREATIVITY

by

Navita Singh

White Falcon Publishing

www.whitefalconpublishing.com

SPARKING CREATIVITY
Navita Singh

www.whitefalconpublishing.com

Picture credits
All photographs have been clicked by the author.
All the pictures of Art and Craft projects including the
cover belong to the author.

Art and Craft credits
The craft work, paintings, sketches and other art work have
been created by the author. Some of the crafts are done by
her students under her guidance.

Requests for permission should be addressed to
navitabsingh@gmail.com

ISBN – 978-93-89932-05-8

CONTENTS

To the Artist in every child

INTRODUCTION

My association with Art and Craft has been since early childhood. I grew up in an artistic environment at home. School provided an opportunity to learn various crafts. College was an immensely creative phase with exposure to new ideas and techniques. From practising architecture, it was by chance that I ventured into mentoring children in Art and Craft. It has been 7 years since I started KREATIVE KIDZ. During this period, I have helped the kids to do numerous Art and Craft projects. Over the years this led to a large collection of projects which inspired me to compile some of them into a book.

I thought of making this book more stimulating by adding some interesting facts and useful tips.

Working with children is a pleasant, relaxing and fulfilling experience. All children have an artist in them that just needs to be discovered. It is good to engage them in Art and Craft activities in early childhood.

Young kids are willing to absorb fresh ideas and learn new techniques. Their imagination is uninhibited, refreshing and fascinating. They get immense joy and satisfaction in creating their own work of Art.

Introducing children to Art and Craft at a tender age

• helps to develop fine motor skills

- builds confidence
- boosts creativity
- stimulates imagination
- encourages experimentation
- cultivates aesthetic appreciation.

A few craft papers, scissors and adhesive are all that is required to get them started. At times, even trash lying around the house is enough to fire their imagination. There is no need to spend on expensive craft items or kits. Simple everyday things can be used to create beautiful crafts.

The crafts in this book require simple materials and basic drawing, cutting, folding and sticking skills. Young children will need the help of an adult to do these craft projects.

This book is ideal for children of all ages to be creatively engaged in their spare time. I am extremely grateful to my dear family for their constant support and encouragement which was instrumental in making this book possible.

– Navita Singh

PRETTY FLOWERS

MATERIALS

- Craft paper
- Drinking straw
- Green cello tape / green craft paper
- Small paper cup
- Florist's sponge
- Cello tape
- Sketch pens
- Glitter pens
- Scissors

TIP

You can use wooden stick for stem and a small glass for the flower pot.

METHOD

- Draw out the flower in Figure 1 on a craft paper of your choice.
- Cut out the flower and decorate it with sketch pens and glitter pens.

- Take green cello tape or 1cm wide strip of green craft paper.
- Starting at an angle cover the straw with the green tape or paper.
- Cut out a green leaf and stick to the straw stem.
- With cello tape attach the stem to the backside of the flower.
- Now, take a piece of florist's sponge and fit it in the cup.
- Make the straw stem stand firmly in this sponge.
- Make more flowers of different colours and shapes to brighten your room.

Figure 1

- Some flowers like roses are edible. They can be used in preparing dishes and drinks.
- The annual flower parade of Holland is the most spectacular in the world.
- Some flowers like those of bougainvillea are actually coloured leaves.
- The Rafflesia Aronoldii is the largest flower in the world. It is found in the rainforests of Indonesia.

It is a parasitic plant and can grow up to 3' in diameter.

Water colour painting of Irises by the author

SHINING STARS

MATERIALS

- Craft paper
- Silver paper
- Thick card
- Thick string
- Adhesive
- Scissors

METHOD

- Draw the five-pointed star as in figure 2 on the thick card.
- Cut out the star.
- Using this star as a stencil, trace out 2 stars on silver paper. Cut them out.

Figure 2

- Trace out the inner star from figure 2 on the coloured craft paper twice. Cut out the two stars.

- Using adhesive stick silver paper star on one side of the thick card star. On top of the silver paper star stick the coloured paper star.
- Insert a piece of string between the thick card and the silver paper stars before repeating the above step on the other side of the card.
- Let it dry for a while.
- Your star decoration is ready!
- You can make several colourful stars to adorn your home.

- Stars twinkle but planets do not.
- The sun is a star around which the planets revolve.
- There are billions of galaxies in the universe and each galaxy has billions of stars.
- The North star or Pole star has been used in navigation since ancient times.
- The morning and evening star, Venus, is actually the brightest planet that is visible before sunrise and sunset.

BOLD BOOKMARKS

MATERIALS

- Thick card
- Craft paper (3 colours)
- Coloured thread/ribbon
- Glitter pens
- Sketch pens
- Adhesive
- Paper punch
- Scissors

METHOD

- Cut a thick card into a rectangle of 4cmX15cm.
- Select 3 colours of craft paper that form a good scheme.
- Follow Figure 3 on how to use these 3 colours.
- Cut the first craft paper for the base and wrap the card rectangle in it.
- Stick it well with adhesive.
- Take the second craft paper and cut a square of 3cmx3cm.

- Stick it towards the top of the rectangular piece leaving 2cm space for punching a hole, and equal margins on the sides.
- Take the third craft paper and cut a rectangle of 3cm x 9 cm.
- Stick it below the square leaving equal margins of 0.5 cm all around.
- On the square piece, draw out a star or any other pattern with sketch pens and glitter pens.

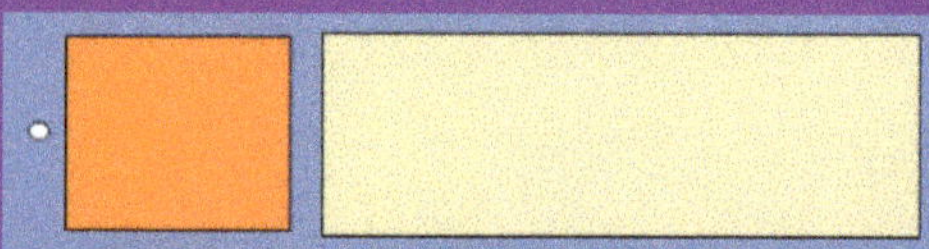

Figure 3

- On the rectangular piece, write your name in a font of your choice. Highlight with sketch pens and glitter pens.
- Now punch a hole 1 cm from the top.
- Tie the coloured thread through it.
- Your beautiful bookmark is ready to

use when you read
your next book.

WHY YOU SHOULD READ BOOKS?

Books are important as they not only increase knowledge but also

- are a source of inspiration
- help to improve vocabulary and language
- fire your imagination
- teach you a lot about life
- introduce new ideas, thoughts and views

- help build concentration
- promote curiosity and discussion
- make you less dependent on electronic gadgets.

Use your imagination to make other designs for book marks

TINY HUT

MATERIALS

- White paper cup
- Craft paper
- Sketch pens
- Colour pencils
- Adhesive
- Scissors

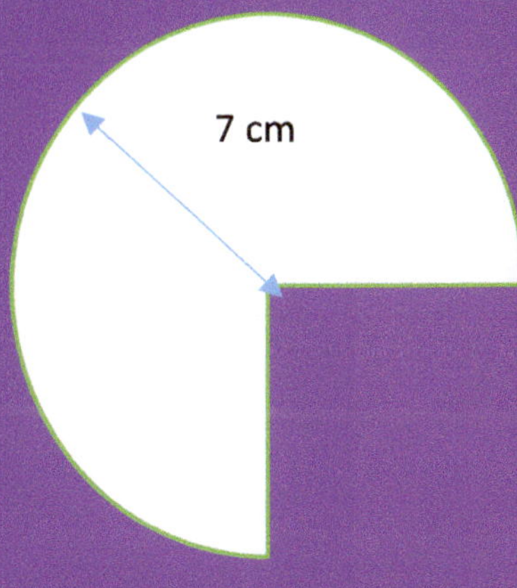

Figure 4

METHOD

- For the roof take a coloured craft paper of your choice.
- Draw Figure 4 on this paper and cut it out.
- With black sketch pen, draw out the pattern of tiles on it.
- Bring together the sides to form a cone and stick with adhesive.
- Now on the paper cup, draw a door, windows and brick/stone pattern.

- Use sketch pens and colour pencils to fill the pattern.
- With adhesive, stick the roof on the paper cup base.
- Your cute little hut is ready!
- Make a few more huts to create a small village.

WHY HAVE A GREEN HOME?

A green home is one that

- does least harm to nature while building it
- does not pollute the environment
- uses natural and local materials
- uses less water and electricity
- is designed to suit the climate so that little or no artificial heating or cooling is needed
- uses natural resources like rain water and solar energy.

A streetscape in water colours by the author

BREEZY WINDMILL

MATERIALS

- Large paper cup
- Thick card
- Acrylic/Poster paints
- Brushes
- Coloured thumbtack
- Glitter pen
- Scissors

Figure 5

METHOD

- Paint the paper cup in a colour of your choice and let it dry.
- Paint a door and a window.
- Draw the cross shape as in figure 5 on a piece of thick card to form the fan of the windmill.
- Cut it out and paint it in a colour contrasting the paper cup base.
- Let it dry and then draw lines with glitter pen across the blades of the fan to complete the detailing.

- Fix the fan with a colourful thumbtack passing through its middle and into the top of the paper cup base.
- Brighten your room with these colourful windmills.

DID YOU KNOW?

- Windmills first came into existence in 2000 BC in Persia.
- In ancient times they were mainly used for grinding flour or pumping water.
- Today they are mostly used to generate power.

- Wind is a free, renewable and an eco-friendly source of energy.
- Netherlands is home to the largest number of ancient windmills.

BEAUTIFUL BANGLES

MATERIALS

- Craft paper
- Glitter tapes
- Cello tape
- Adhesive
- Scissors

METHOD

- Take a 12.5 cm wide strip of coloured craft paper.
- Fold it along the width at 2 cm.
- Fold it again in a continuous way over the first 2 cm wide fold.
- Finally, there is a thick 2 cm paper strip.
- Apply adhesive to the final fold and stick it.
- Now take a glitter tape of your choice.
- Stick the tape at an angle on the paper strip and begin to wind it.
- Continue till the full strip is covered with this diagonal pattern of the glitter tape.

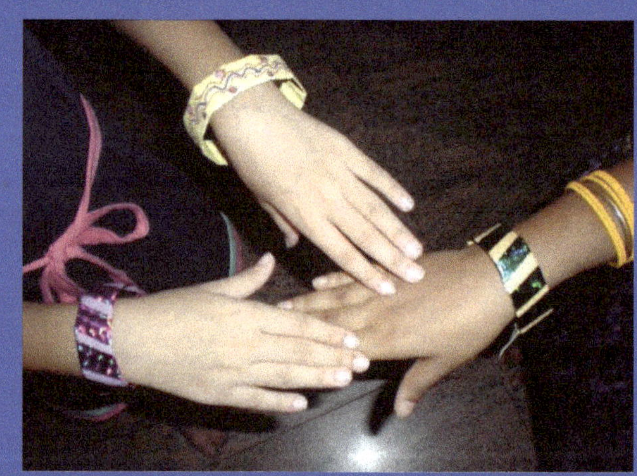

- You can use sketch pens or glitter pens to further decorate the bangle.
- Bring the ends of this strip together and secure it firmly with a cello tape.
- Your designer bangle is ready for you to flaunt!

MAKE PAPER JEWELLERY

Instead of expensive metals or stones, jewellery can be made of paper.

Paper jewellery is

- Unique
- Creative
- Handmade
- Inexpensive
- Colourful
- Environment-friendly
- Light weight.

TIPS

- Use adhesive or varnish to make paper jewellery strong and water proof.
- Experiment with different designs.
- Make a variety of jewellery to go with your outfits.
- Add beads and gem stones for making jewellery more attractive.

Paper jewellery using quilling technique

SUNFLOWER BADGE

MATERIALS

- Yellow craft paper
- Orange craft paper
- Thick card
- Glitter pens
- Sequins
- Gemstone
- Safety pin
- Adhesive
- Cello tape
- Scissors

TIP

You can use any colour or pattern to create more flower badges.

METHOD

- Draw a sunflower each on yellow and orange craft paper.
- Stick the orange paper on the thick card with adhesive.
- Cut out the sunflower.
- Now, cut out the yellow sunflower also.
- With glitter pen, draw the outline for both the flowers.
- Decorate the yellow flower with gemstone and sequins.
- Paste the yellow flower on the orange flower in

a way that petals are staggered.

- The orange sunflower petals should show behind the yellow sunflower.
- At the back of the orange flower attach a safety pin with cello tape.
- Now, you can wear your sunflower badge to brighten up your shirt or dress.
- Don't be surprised when heads turn to see your new accessory!

DID YOU KNOW?

- Sunflower's scientific name is *Helianthus*, Helia for sun and anthus for flower.
- Sunflower is not a single flower but a collection of many flowers.

- The centre has the real flowers whereas the petals are only false ones only for attractive display.

- Sunflowers are used to produce oils, snacks and bird seed.

- Sunflower is the national flower of Ukraine.

- Each flower can grow up to 3m in height and produce around 2000 seeds.

- Young sunflowers face the sun due to a phenomenon called Heliotropism.

Water colour painting by the author

MOSAIC FISH

MATERIALS

- Craft paper (3 colours)
- Blue paper
- Black paper
- Thick card
- Piece of thick string
- Cello tape
- Adhesive
- Double sticking tape
- Scissors

METHOD

- Draw out the fish on a piece of thick card.
- Tear the 3 coloured craft paper into small pieces and keep them separately.
- Apply adhesive on the body of the fish.
- Use separate colours for the fins and tail, face and rest of the body.
- Paste the pieces of colour paper carefully covering every part of the fish.
- Use more adhesive wherever required.
- Keep it aside to dry.

- Take a piece of 10 cm x 10 cm thick card.
- Paste black paper on it.
- Draw a border with a glitter pen.
- Make a loop of thick string and fix it firmly at the back of the card with cello tape.
- Now, cut out the fish from the thick card.
- Use a piece of double sticking tape to fix it onto the black background.
- Tear some blue paper to form waves.
- Stick them on the black paper around the fish.
- Your beautiful mosaic fish is ready to decorate your home!

DID YOU KNOW?

- Dolphins and whales are not fishes but mammals.
- They do not lay eggs but young ones.
- They do not use gills for breathing. They have lungs so have to come up to take air.

Glass painting of Dolphins by the author

- Dolphins communicate through various sounds and whistling.
- They are very social and live in groups called pods.
- Hector's dolphin is the smallest sea mammal in the world.

Seascape by author using Fluid Art

FRIDGE MAGNETS

MATERIALS

- Foam sheet (3 colours)
- Magnets (3)
- Card board
- Decorative gems
- Adhesive
- Scissors

METHOD

- Draw and cut out 3 squares of cardboard 5cm x 5cm.
- Using these squares as stencils cut out squares of different coloured foam sheets.
- Stick them each on a cardboard square.
- Stick one magnet on the back side of each square piece.
- Cut out a star, heart and flower as shown in the picture below. For the flower cut out each petal separately.
- Stick them on different coloured square backgrounds.

- Decorate with the sparkling gems.
- Elegant fridge magnets are ready to adorn your dining room or kitchen!

DID YOU KNOW?

- The earth behaves like a large magnet.
- A magnet has a North and a South pole.
- A compass has a magnetic needle to find direction.
- When two magnets are placed end to end their like poles repel and unlike poles attract.
- Electromagnets are those that turn into magnets only when supplied with electric current.
- Electromagnets are used in door bells, telephones, microphones, loudspeakers, etc.
- Maglev trains are very fascinating as they have no wheels but hover above the tracks due to magnetic repulsion.
- Magnets can be used to make interesting crafts that can stick to metal surfaces.

Interesting floral fridge magnets made by quilling

TOY TORTOISE

MATERIALS

- Yellow craft paper
- Green craft paper
- Sketch pens
- Adhesive
- Scissors

METHOD

- Cut a circle of 7cm radius out of green craft paper.
- Make a cut along the radius to the centre.
- Adjust the two ends along the cut to form a shallow cone.
- Stick the ends in this position.
- With black sketch pen draw the pattern for the shell.
- Cut out four rectangles 2.5cmx3.5 cm from yellow craft paper.
- Draw curves at one end of each rectangle.
- Cut it out to form the legs.
- Draw the toes in black sketch pen.
- Fix the four legs symmetrically under the green shell.
- Draw and cut out the face from yellow craft paper.
- Complete the eyes and mouth with black sketch pen.

- Draw and cut out a triangular tail.
- Cut two slits diagonally on the green shell to fix the face and tail.
- Now, it is time to play with your toy tortoise that you have created!

DID YOU KNOW?

- Tortoise is a cold-blooded land-dwelling reptile.
- It has a hard shell covering its body.
- Some tortoises can retract their feet and head to protect themselves.
- Tortoise has only a horny mouth and no teeth.
- It does not have any external ears but only holes for hearing.
- Tortoises hibernate in winters.
- Adwaita, a giant tortoise lived up to the age of 250 years in a Calcutta zoo.

PENCIL STAND

MATERIALS

- Craft paper
- Glitter tape
- Gem stones
- Sequins
- Adhesive
- Scissors
- Used paper roll
- Cutter
- Sketch pens
- Glitter pens
- Crayons

METHOD

- Take a used paper roll
  and mark a line at a
  height of 10 cm. Cut it
  out with a cutter.

- Take a 10 cm wide
  piece of your choice of
  craft paper.
- Roll it around the
  paper roll with at least
  1 cm overlap. Cut out
  this much craft paper.

- Take glitter tape and stick it at the top rim and bottom edge of the craft paper piece.
- Draw flowers or any other pattern on the craft paper.
- Colour and decorate with sketch pens, crayons, glitter pens, gem stones and sequins.
- Make the kitchen paper roll stand and trace out the circular base on a piece of card.
- Cut it out and fix it to the bottom of the roll with the help of adhesive.
- Finally apply adhesive on the backside of the decorated craft paper and stick it around the paper roll.
- A beautiful pencil stand is ready for you to organise your stationery!

A beautiful candle holder made by using an old CD

Stained glass lamp from old glass jar that won the Green Champion award for the author

UPCYCLING: A CREATIVE SOLUTION

Upcycling is reusing waste without destroying it to form something more useful and beautiful.

Upcycling has several advantages

- encourages creative reuse
- less trash or garbage generated
- saves money on buying a new product
- eco-friendly as it minimises pollution of land, water and air
- conserves energy that is used for making a new product.

For craft activities try to use waste products and materials.

- Instead of buying cardboard use cartons of the cereals and snacks.
- Use plastic bottles to create various kinds of holders and containers.
- Use toilet and kitchen rolls to make useful and interesting items like pencil stands, toys, decor items, etc.
- Reuse plastic containers for growing small plants.
- Use old newspaper and magazines to make papier-mache items or weave baskets.
- Decorate cardboard boxes to organise and store things.

An interesting hanging planter from plastic bottle

CUTE PUPPET

MATERIALS

FOR PUPPET

- A large ice cream stick
- A small ice cream stick
- A lid of some bottle/jar (5 cm diameter)
- Googly eyes
- Black wool
- Craft paper
- Acrylic paints
- Paintbrush
- Sketch pens
- Glitter pens
- Scissors
- Adhesive

METHOD

- Trace out the lid on a light-coloured craft paper.
- Draw out the puppet's face.
- Paint the two ice cream sticks in a colour your choice.
- Let them dry.
- Stick the longer ice cream stick behind the lid to form the body.
- Stick the face onto the lid.
- Stick the googly eyes.
- Now for the arms, stick the smaller ice cream

stick across the longer
one.

- Draw out clothes for
  the puppet on craft
  paper. Colour and
  decorate them.
- Stick the clothes on the
  ice cream stick so that
  the arms pass through
  the sleeves.
- For the hair, fold some
  length of black wool to
  form a bundle.
- Tie it up in the middle
  and cut the edges to
  form the strands of
  hair.
- Stick it on top of the
  head.

- Your endearing little
  puppet is ready!

Another delightful puppet!

Make a few more puppets with a variety of dresses and hairstyles to stage your own puppet show.

For your puppet show you can create a cute little theatre for performance.

MATERIALS
FOR THEATRE
- Cardboard box
- Piece of cloth for curtains
- Ribbon

METHOD
- Take a cardboard box around 3.5 cm in height.
- Cut out the bottom to form an opening

leaving 2.5 cm frame around the edges.

Your little puppet theatre

- Decorate the front frame and the sides after painting or sticking craft paper.
- Make it stand on its longer side at the edge of a table.

- Make curtains with old cloth and attach to the sides.
- Arrange a torch or a lamp to light your theatre.
- Take your position behind the theatre.
- Ask your audience to be seated on the opposite side.
- Switch off the lights and turn on a lamp to focus on the stage.
- Now, it is time to begin your very own puppet show.
- Be prepared for a big applause at the end of your performance!

Create more interesting puppets for added fun!

GIFT BAGS

MATERIALS

- Thick textured paper
- Few strips 7mm wide of coloured craft paper
- Satin ribbon
- Adhesive
- A pair of scissors
- A pencil
- Cello tape

METHOD

- Trace out the template in Figure 3 on the textured paper.
- Cut out the shape along the firm lines.
  - Fold along the dotted lines.
- Apply adhesive on shaded part and stick to form a bag.
- Now fold along dashed lines.
- Roll the coloured paper strips onto a pencil.
- Remove and let it uncoil a bit and stick the edges to form circular shapes of assorted colours and sizes.
- Stick these shapes on the bag with adhesive.
- Cut satin ribbon to form two handles for the bag.

- Stick them well with cello tape from the inside.
- Your beautiful bag is ready to carry that special gift!

Handmade box for gifting

SOME GIFTING AND PARTY IDEAS

- Use these gift bags for giving gifts to others and return gifts for your party.
- Make gift tags and wrap the gifts in your own style.
- Use your creativity to make the gift also yourself as it adds a personalised touch.
- Wrap the gift in a paper that you create yourself by drawing, stencilling, printing or painting.

- Select a theme for your party.
- Create your own invitation cards giving details of the date, time and venue.
- Do the party decoration yourself by making your own party banner and buntings.
- Lay the table with cute name cards, special plates, napkins and glasses to complete the theme.
- Innovative games for your party will be a lot of fun for you and your guests.
- These few things will make your party really special!

Make fancy party masks and hats

Figure 6

- Cut along firm lines and fold along dotted lines.
- Apply glue on shaded portions and stick
- Finally, fold inwards along the dashed lines

SOME MORE IDEAS FOR CREATING HANDMADE GIFTS

Below, are two handmade gifts by the author. An elegant photo frame adorned with the Italian Sospeso technique and a golden spray-painted wooden plaque with a free-hand reindeer silhouette drawn and painted on it.

HANDY NOTEPADS

MATERIALS

- Few sheets of paper (ruled or plain)
- Fancy tape
- Glitter tape
- Craft papers
- Glitter pens
- Thick card
- Stapler

METHOD

- Fold the white paper to form rectangles 7.5cm x 10 cm.
- Cut along the folds to form different pages of the notepad.
- Put all the papers in a stack and staple one end.
- Cut thick card to form a continuous back and front cover.
- Fold it into half.
- Take craft paper of your choice and stick on the front and back.
- Now, decorate the front cover.
- Cut out stars from another craft paper and stick using adhesive.
- Use the fancy and glitter tapes to form two lines at the bottom.
- Use glitter pens for further decoration.

- Stick the cover by applying adhesive over the stapled part of the white paper notepad.
- Your personal notepad is ready for use!

HOW TO USE YOUR NOTEPAD

- Make list of things to do.
- Write a shopping list.
- Take notes or draw sketches when you go for a class, meeting or excursion.
- Note down phone numbers and addresses.
- Write messages for your family or friends.
- Make a list of things to carry on a trip.
- Just doodle or play a game with a friend like tic-tac-toe.

JOLLY SANTA

MATERIALS

- Used paper roll
- Red craft paper
- Brown craft paper
- Peach /Orange craft paper
- Googly Eyes
- Cotton
- Scissors
- Adhesive

METHOD

- Take a used paper roll. Cut it around 10 cm length.
- Cover it with red craft paper using adhesive.
- Cut a U-shaped piece of peach/orange craft paper and stick it on the red paper roll to form a face.
- Cut out a semi-circle of red craft paper of 7 cm radius to form a cone for the cap.

- Put a piece of cotton ball on top of the cap.
- Add some cotton strip around the rim at the bottom.

- Use thick strips of cotton on the face to form the beard and moustache.
- Stick googly eyes or draw them out if you do not have ready-to-use ones.
- Stick a thin strip of brown paper to form a belt.
- Draw out a buckle with pen.
- Stick the cap to the base of red paper roll.
- Your Jolly Santa is ready!
- Make your own decorations for X'mas to deck up your home.

Make your own X'mas tree

ABOUT SANTA CLAUS

- The Jolly Old character of Santa Claus was inspired by the benevolent St Nicholas who lived in Turkey in the 3rd century AD. He gave away all his wealth to the poor and sick. He was very fond of children also.
- According to legend, on Xmas eve Santa arrived from his home in the North pole on his sleigh full of gifts. It was driven by flying reindeers one of whom was Rudolph, who had a shiny red nose.
- Santa went down the chimney and put the gifts for good children in the stockings kept by them. However, he would leave only coal for the naughty children.